SOFIA VALDEZ'S
BIG PROJECT BOOK FOR AWESOME ACTIVISTS

by Andrea Beaty   illustrations by David Roberts

Abrams Books for Young Readers
New York

It's a big world with lots of problems to solve.
Just remember:

No one can do everything.
But everyone can do something.

Cataloging-in-Publication Data has been applied for and may be obtained from the Library of Congress.

ISBN 978-1-4197-4944-5

Text copyright © 2021 Andrea Beaty
Illustrations copyright © 2021 David Roberts
Additional illustrations by Noah MacMillan
Book design by Laura Crescenti

Published in 2021 by Abrams Books for Young Readers, an imprint of ABRAMS. All rights reserved.
No portion of this book may be reproduced, stored in a retrieval system, or transmitted in any form
or by any means, mechanical, electronic, photocopying, recording, or otherwise, without written
permission from the publisher.

Printed and bound in U.S.A.
10 9 8 7 6 5 4 3 2 1

Abrams Books for Young Readers are available at special discounts when purchased in quantity for
premiums and promotions as well as fundraising or educational use. Special editions can also be
created to specification. For details, contact specialsales@abramsbooks.com or the address below.

Abrams® is a registered trademark of Harry N. Abrams, Inc.

ABRAMS The Art of Books
195 Broadway, New York, NY 10007
abramsbooks.com

AWESOME ACTIVIST

_____

(your name)

Draw a picture of
yourself here!

THIS BOOK IS FOR YOU.

Use the pages to brainstorm ideas and imagine better ways of doing things. Be creative.
Be bold. And always be kind. Use this book to make a difference in your school, town,
country, and planet. You will learn how communities work. How to connect with
other people. How to become a better listener. A leader. An activist.

THE STORY OF SOFIA VALDEZ, FUTURE PREZ

Even as a baby, Sofia Valdez got things done. She helped Abuelo plant a magnolia tree after her mother died. As she grew older, she went door-to-door with Abuelo to help their elderly neighbors. Sometimes she took their pets for a walk. Or she stopped to chat and keep them company. Sofia always tried to do what she could to help her family, her friends, and her whole neighborhood.

Each day, Abuelo and Pup walked Sofia to school and back home again. One day, Pup saw a squirrel and took off running. Zoom! Pup dragged Abuelo along. Sofia ran to keep up!

Pup ran up, up, up to the top of a hill made of leftover junk for the local landfill. *CRASH!* Mount Trashmore split, and they all tumbled down onto a moldy old pumpkin. *SPLAT!*

"OUCH!" cried Abuelo.

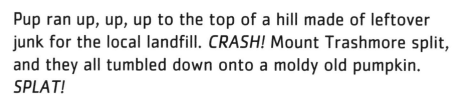

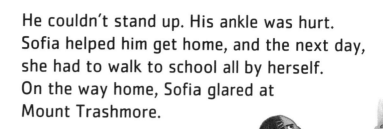

He couldn't stand up. His ankle was hurt.
Sofia helped him get home, and the next day,
she had to walk to school all by herself.
On the way home, Sofia glared at
Mount Trashmore.

"This is not right!" she declared.

Sofia got very angry.

But she also got an idea! Blue River Creek should
get rid of Mount Trashmore and build a new park!
The next morning, Sofia put a sign in her yard.

Sofia asked her neighbors what they thought.
They all had wonderful ideas for the park.
Sofia wrote them all down. That night, she
made a plan for the park and went to bed.
In the middle of the night—*BAM!*—
a thought woke her up. She realized
that everyone had asked her
to let them know when the
park was done.

They all thought that Sofia
could make the park by
herself. How could one
person do that?

She was so worried that she tossed and turned for a long time. Finally, she slept. In the morning, Sofia was sad when she saw Abuelo's hurt ankle. Even if nobody else would help, she had to try to build a park. Abuelo gave her a hug and a bag of cookies for luck.

All by herself, Sofia Valdez went to face City Hall.

At City Hall, she went to the mayor's office, which sent her to the Department of Fun, which sent her to the Office of Duck Ponds and Cool Things to Do. That department sent her to the Office of Monkeys, which sent her to the Department of Cheese, which sent her to the Division of Fountains and Meetings and Bees. At last, Sofia was sent to the basement to see Clerk Clara Clark.

Clerk Clark looked at her. "You can't build a new park," she said. "You're only a kid!"

Sofia was shocked! She didn't know what to do.

"I think that law's wrong!" she said, though her voice didn't sound strong.

"It can't be done," said the clerk. "Do you have any questions?"

Sofia held up the picture of Abuelo.

"If he was your grandpa," she said. "What would you do?"

Clerk Clark thought and thought. Then, she called in everybody who worked at City Hall. They all crammed into the office and leaned toward Sofia to hear what she had to say. She was nervous and worried. But she had to help Abuelo! She tried to speak, but she couldn't find her voice.

They leaned even closer and Sofia leaned back. At that moment, her arm brushed the edge of the bag of cookies Abuelo had given her. It made her think of Abuelo and how he was hurt.

At that moment, Sofia knew that she had to speak up. She knew that being brave meant doing the thing she must do, even if it was scary.

Sofia took a deep breath. Then, she told them why she was there. She told them about Abuelo and their neighbors and the park. Once she got talking, it was easier and easier.

At last, the Mayor told her to start a petition and if enough people signed it, they would try to make the park. Sofia got right to work.

At first, only a few people helped, but then, others saw what they were doing, and they helped too! It took a long time and a lot of work, but finally, Blue River Creek got a new park for everyone!

The people of Blue River Creek think that someday, Sofia Valdez could grow up to be president. But for now, she spends her time doing what she loves most: helping Blue River Creek get better and better.

ACTIVIST'S TREASURES
AND TOOLS

FRIENDS

HEART

BOOKS

NOTEBOOKS

NEWSPAPERS

**POSTER-MAKING
SUPPLIES**

TELEPHONE

BUTTONS

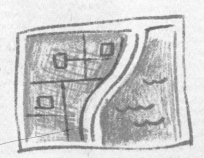

MAP

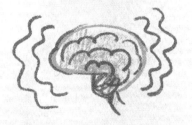

BRAIN

COMPUTER

EARS

LIBRARY CARD

LIST TOPICS THAT ARE IMPORTANT TO YOU

The Environment
_____

The Planet
_____

Animals
_____

My Family
_____

Equality
_____

Justice
_____

Other Kids
_____

School
_____

_____

_____

_____

_____

Sign our Petition Please

Si, Se Puede!

Can you find all the words listed to the right in the puzzle below?

(In case you need help, the answer key can be found on page 94.)

```
A T R Q T A P X B R A V E O N J
C G F S G E N E R O U S T E L I
N E W S P A P E R C I V B L I E
C O N V E R S A T I O N T U S S
Q O K C R S L P T I J Y O F T H
J W Q E H O Z L E M D H C S E S
X E M L A C T I V I S T A L N O
C R U E W I O A I E R W U Y E V
A T E X O A A M Y M I N A L R H
L M Z T P L W V M A Y O R G Y D
A I T D E G V O L U N T E E R S
L E A D E R O R Z R N Q K O E D
Q C V N A O C L V A O I U Q A M
T O H T U U A E N G I E T X D A
V E U C X P G E M P A T H Y M Y
T H E F R E E P R E S S B Y L H
```

Activist
Activism
Community
Government
Vote
Leader
Generous
Mayor

Inspiring
Budget
Taxes
Listener
Conversation
Communication
Kindness
Volunteer

Read
Question
Think
Informed
Newspaper
Journalist
The Free Press
Social Group

Brave
Patient
Creative
Vigilant
Humble
Empathy

```
C O M M U N I C A T I O N O T R
S F K C R E A T I V E A L S U L
N T L O L A C H L H R I C A P I
G L L R A S T B U D G E T O N N
M I A M N K I N D N E S S Q I S
E R C A G O V E R N M E N T U P
R C A P R N I A W X Q S H F I
C O F A Y H S N A U C T P I O R
N F N T K R M Y F L R O N N V I
M C J I Y P V H E O I S Y K O N
T A X E S L W S R Q R I C A T G
O U R N A L I S T H J M U J E C
K W E T H N C E K P Q E E B G T
C E S D P B P L R A W B S D M Z
B F N O L V I G I L A N T N Y Z
R H U M B L E P Q U E S T I O N
```

YOU ARE HERE.

You live on the Planet Earth in our Solar System in the Milky Way in the Universe.

There are other people on Planet Earth, too.
About 7.7 BILLION of them! The number looks
like this: 7,763,961,456 and it grows every second.
Oops. Now it's 7,763,961,494 . . . oops!
Now it's 7,763,961,743 . . . oops! . . . Now it's . . .

That is a lot of people. And they are all different!
No two people on Earth are exactly alike.

Draw a picture of you and where you live.

Draw a person who is completely different
from you. Think about where they live.
What they look like. How they dress.
What they do. What they eat. How they
speak. The music they love. Their family.
Their pets.

Put a check by each of the things on this list that you need.

Put a heart by each of the things on this list that the other person needs.

Think about it: What other things are important to you? To the other person? What would you add to this list?

	✓	♥
AIR		
WATER		
FOOD		
WARMTH		
SLEEP		
CLOTHES		
SHELTER		
SAFETY		
$ TO PAY FOR FOOD & SHELTER		
EDUCATION		
LOVE		
KINDNESS		
FREEDOM		
FRIENDS		
FAMILY		
CAKE		
HAPPINESS		
PRIVACY		
LAUGHTER		
EQUALITY AND JUSTICE		
EQUAL ACCESS TO PUBLIC SPACES		
THE ABILITY TO COMMUNICATE		
INFORMATION		
RIGHT TO GET TOGETHER WITH OTHERS		

SOCIAL ANIMALS

Some animals live together with others of their species in complicated social groups. A pod of whales. A pack of wolves. A herd of elephants. A hive of bees.

Members have their own roles in the group, and they behave in ways that benefit the whole group. This social structure helps the group stay safe, protect the young, and find basic needs such as food, water, and shelter.

Other animals live most of their lives alone and connect with others only to mate and raise their young. Skunks, leopards, moles, sloths, wolverines, and bears are solitary animals.

We don't usually think about it, but people are social animals. Family, friends, and community are very important to us. But what if they weren't?

Imagine if humans were solitary animals. If you lived most of your life by yourself, how would you find food? Where would you live? What would you do for fun?

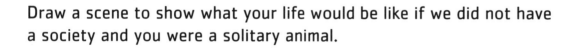

Draw a scene to show what your life would be like if we did not have a society and you were a solitary animal.

Humans organize into many social groups. Think about the many social groups in your life: your family, friends, classroom, school, neighborhood, town, region, nation, humankind.

Draw a picture of a group to which you belong. What do you love about this group?

Each kind of social group makes decisions in its own way and decides on the rules for the group.

For instance, the adults in a family might set rules for the children. The school board, principal, and teachers might set the rules for a school. The people of a town might vote as a group to make decisions that affect everyone who lives there. Or, they might elect a few people to make those decisions for the whole town.

Sometimes, social rules are written down as official guidelines or laws. Sometimes, social rules are suggestions for the best behavior or for accepted good manners.

Think about your school. What are some of the rules that students and adults follow? What are the good behaviors that are encouraged but which are not official rules?

If you were the head of your school, what kind of rules would you want to make in order to help everyone get along, get things done, respect each other, learn, and be safe? List them here.

YOUR SCHOOL RULES

_____

_____

_____

_____

_____

_____

_____

_____

_____

_____

FAMILY RULES AND ROLES

Think about your family. How are rules made in your family? What are some rules in your family? What jobs need to be done in your family? Which jobs do you do? Can you help other people in your family with their jobs?

Draw a picture of your family doing chores.

LIST YOUR CHORES OR WAYS YOU HELP YOUR FAMILY.

_____   _____

_____   _____

_____   _____

_____   _____

WHAT DOES AN ACTIVIST DO?

When Abuelo got hurt, Sofia wanted to help. She decided that a park in Blue River Creek would help Abuelo and others who needed a safe place to gather.

Activists think about others and try to improve their community, country, or planet. They see a problem and ask, **"HOW CAN I HELP?"**

There is always a way to help. Activists use their talents, hearts, hard work, and time to help others.

Look around your community. Think about ways you can help. They could be physical things like better roads or sidewalks. They could be social things like having more connection between different kinds of people. Ask others what they think about the community and changes they would like to see.

THE PLACE WHERE YOU LIVE: _____

Things you love about your community	Things that could be improved in your community

ACTIVISTS ARE INSPIRING

Nobody can do everything by themselves. It takes lots of help to make changes in a community. Just standing up and trying to make a difference can inspire others. That's how Sofia inspired her family and Clerk Clara Clark to help build support for a new park. Together, they inspired others like Miss Greer and the kids in Grade Two!

Think about someone who inspires you. Draw their picture here.

ACTIVISTS HAVE EMPATHY

Empathy is the ability to understand the feelings of others.
One of the best ways to create a strong sense of empathy is to read.
Reading books helps you look at the world through the eyes of the book's
characters and imagine what it might be like to face the situations they face.
It lets you feel the emotions the characters experience and imagine what
it would be like to be someone else.

The more you read, the better you will
understand the world and the people in it.

KEEP TRACK OF THE BOOKS YOU READ!

BOOK TITLE	COMMENTS ABOUT THE BOOK

How did the book make you feel? How did you feel similar to the characters? How did you feel different? What did you learn?

19

ACTIVISTS WORK TOGETHER

Working as a team is fun, but it can also be a challenge. Some basic rules help teams work smoothly.

- Listen and ask questions.

- Respect other people's opinions, talents, and time!

- Be open to new points of view. There are many ways to solve most problems. Your solution might not be the best way. If others disagree with your ideas, it does not mean that they reject you!

- Brainstorming is about collecting all ideas—even the weird ones. When brainstorming, never say "No!" to an idea. Instead, say, "Let's think about it." Then think about it! Sometimes the weirdest ideas help you find the best answer.

- Be flexible. Give other people's ideas a chance.

- Don't be a time hog. Let others take turns.

Working as a team doesn't mean that you will all agree completely on a solution. That's okay. Go with the idea that most people can support. Give it a try. Then see how it can be improved.

DRAW A PICTURE OF YOUR TEAM. IT CAN HAVE PEOPLE
YOU KNOW AND ALSO PEOPLE YOU IMAGINE.

 # CITIZENS' PARK

Sofia wanted the new park to meet the needs of all the citizens of Blue River Creek. She asked her neighbors about the park. They had lots to say. They wanted benches, fountains, and places to play. Meeting spots. Gardens. A basket for bees. A rubber duck pond. And a kiosk for cheese. (A kiosk is a small hut where things are sold.) Can you draw Sofia's park here? Include features you might like in your community park.

CITY HALL

Sofia Valdez went to City Hall to try to get a park for Blue River Creek. She went to the Department of Fun and the Office of Duck Ponds and Cool Things to Do. Then, she went to the Office of Monkeys. The Department of Cheese. The Division of Fountains and Meetings and Bees!

Most towns do not have an Office of Monkeys or a Division of Bees. But they have lots of departments and professional people to help the citizens of the town. People in the government are your neighbors and fellow members of the community who work hard to make your town run well. They might be elected by the community, or they might be hired for their job. They are paid by the rest of the community through taxes. Taxes pay people who work for the government, and they also pay for buildings, roads, schools, services like the police and fire department, and so many other things.

If you live in a village, town, or city, chances are that you have a local government that is involved in all kinds of things that affect you and your family!

Think about the following list of items. Who do you think makes them possible in your community? Discuss with an adult to learn about how things work in your community.

CIRCLE THE THINGS THAT YOUR LOCAL GOVERNMENT DEALS WITH:

LIBRARY   CUPCAKES   SIDEWALKS   SEWER LINES   CLEAN WATER   CLEAN AIR

ROAD MAINTENANCE   POLICE   FIREFIGHTERS   CITIZENSHIP CLASSES

CHOCOLATE BARS   AMBULANCE   PARKS   SEVERE WEATHER   ALERTS   VOTING

VACCINATIONS   PIZZA   TRAFFIC CONTROL   COMMUNITY HEALTH   COOKIES   SCHOOLS

GOVERNMENT   BUILDING MAINTENANCE   WILDLIFE PEST CONTROL   DOG CATCHERS

MOSQUITO CONTROL   PARADES   STOP SIGNS   MENTAL HEALTH RESOURCES

BUBBLE GUM   FIREWORKS   EMERGENCY EVACUATION IN CASE OF DISASTER   PUPPIES

HULA HOOPS   PARKING   TRASH PICKUP   STREET LIGHTS   BUSES

Can you think of other ways your government helps you and your family?

YOUR GOVERNMENT

Find out about the local government of your city, town, village, or county.
What departments are there? Who are the leaders of the government? How do they get
that job? Reach out to an elected official in your town or on your school board.

Interview them using these questions and any other questions you'd like to ask.

1. What do you do in your job?

2. Why did you decide to run or apply for this position?

3. Why is it important for people to be involved in their community and run for office?

4. What is the hardest part about your job?

5. What is your favorite part about your job?

6. What is your day like?

7. If you were elected, what is it like to run a campaign? How did other people help you in your election race?

8. How can kids help in our town?

WRITE MORE QUESTIONS HERE:

_____

_____

_____

_____

_____

City governments hold meetings, which are open to the public. Go to a meeting and learn how your government works. The decisions made in your local government will affect you and your family and friends. Learn all you can.

WHERE YOU LIVE

Name of your town or city:

_____

Draw a picture of your town.

Draw a picture of your town with the improvements you'd like to make.

KNOW YOUR SCHOOL

Think about your school. You probably spend a lot of time there, but what do you know about how it works? Here are some questions. See if you can find answers. (Hint: Your teacher or school librarian can help you get started!)
Do you have other questions? Make notes about what you learn.

Who is the head of the school? Who helps them run the school?

How many teachers are there?

What other kind of jobs do people do in the school?

What education, training, or experience is required to become a teacher?

Who hires teachers?

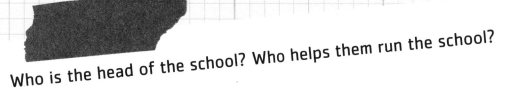

28

Teachers work very hard in the classroom. But they also work hard planning lessons, grading papers, running student clubs, consulting with parents, and even continuing their own education. Ask your teacher about their job.

Where does the money come from to pay teachers?

Is there a school board or group of citizens who makes decisions about schools in your town? Are they elected?

Who helps keep the school clean and fixes things when they break? What are their names?

Can you go to a meeting of the school board or contact a member of the board to learn more?

How can you help your school run more smoothly?

DRAW A PICTURE OF YOUR SCHOOL OR CLASSROOM.

KNOW YOUR COMMUNITY

Now find an adult outside of your school who you might interview.
This could include a city hall clerk, mayor, firefighter, maintenance worker,
food pantry manager, League of Women Voters volunteer, bus driver,
or anyone else you're interested in.

Ask questions like:

- Can you describe your job?

- What is your typical day like?

- How did you start doing this job?

- What is surprising about your job?

- Why is your job important?

- What works well in our community?

- What problems do you see in the community that need work?

- How can kids help?

ADD YOUR OWN QUESTIONS HERE:

Draw a picture of this person doing their job.

THE FUTURE IS GLORG!

Imagine you live in the distant future. Humans travel the stars and settle on new planets. It's your job to design a brand-new town on the planet Glorg! Draw your town below.

Remember to include the City Hall, library, schools, houses, fire station, and other things that citizens of your future space town might need. Think about how citizens will travel in the town.

As you design your town, think about ALL the kinds of people who will live there. A society only works when it works for everyone. That includes people who might not have power, money, or a voice in decision making. How can you include them in the process of governing? In the physical spaces of the town?

THE FUTURE IS GLORG!

Imagine a park for your new town on Glorg.
What would you include?

Draw it here. Remember to think about all the people who might live in your town and any special features they might like or need.

Does your park include awesome places for people of all ages to gather?
Are there places to play that are accessible to all, including those who might have
special needs for seeing, hearing, or getting around? Are pets welcome in the park?
Do they have special places to play?

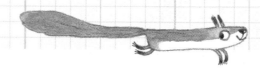

35

THE GOVERNMENT ON GLORG

Your town on Glorg needs a government to help with things the people need—education, clean water, and roads, to name a few. Think about these questions and make notes about your plans.

WHAT IS THE NAME OF YOUR TOWN ON GLORG?

_____

WHAT IS IMPORTANT TO YOU AND THE OTHER CITIZENS ON GLORG?

DO YOU WANT A SINGLE LEADER OR A GROUP OF LEADERS?

WILL YOU HAVE ELECTIONS TO CHOOSE LEADERS?

◯ YES

◯ NO

HOW OFTEN WILL YOU HAVE ELECTIONS?

WHAT KIND OF RULES (LAWS) WOULD YOU INCLUDE ON GLORG?

_____

_____

_____

_____

WHO CAN RUN FOR LEADER?

_____

_____

_____

_____

WHO WOULD DECIDE IF THOSE RULES WERE FAIR?

WHAT WOULD HAPPEN IF LEADERS BROKE THE RULES? WOULD THE LEADER HAVE TO ANSWER TO THE CITIZENS? IF SO, HOW?

COULD THE RULES EVER BE CHANGED? HOW?

FLAGS AND SEALS

Countries, states, provinces, and cities often choose symbols or words to represent ideas that are important to them. These symbols might be included in a city seal or on a flag in City Hall.

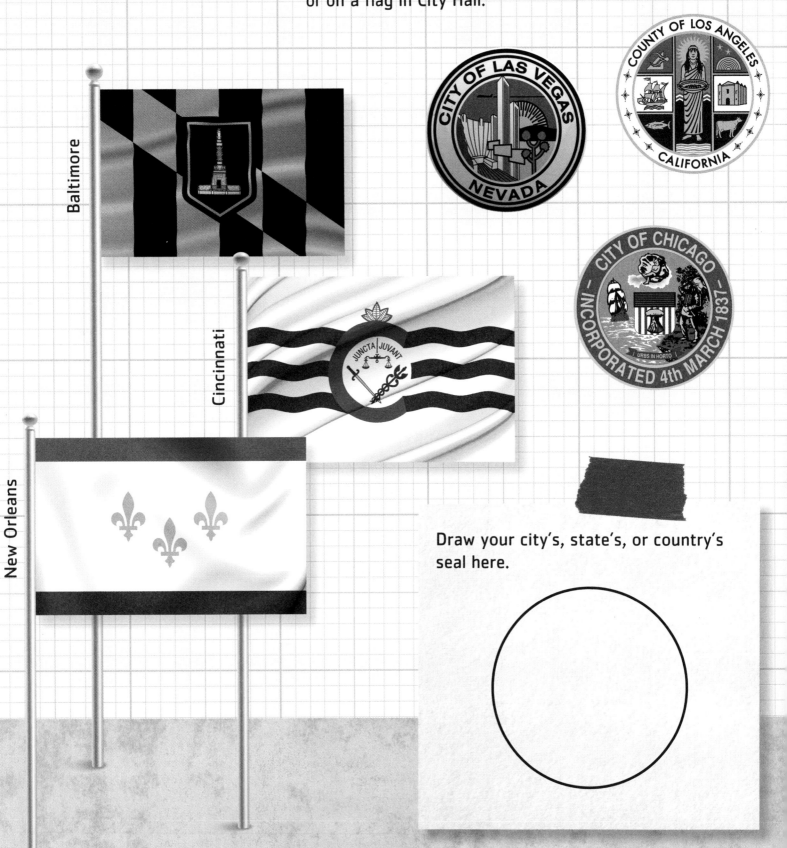

Baltimore

Cincinnati

New Orleans

Draw your city's, state's, or country's seal here.

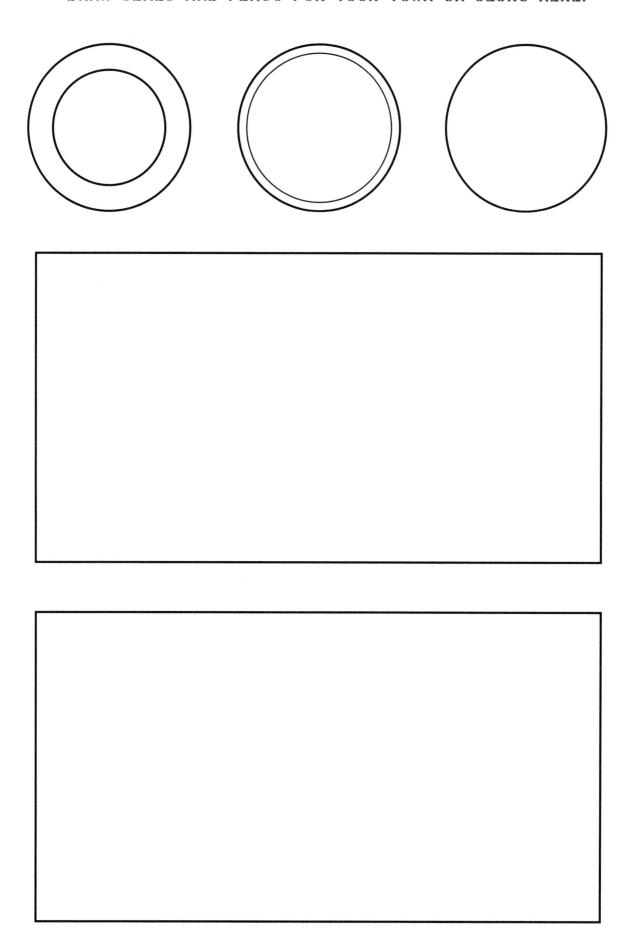

REAL-WORLD PROBLEMS

Education gives people the chance to better understand the world and to discover their talents. Without education, people suffer from poverty and many health and social problems that come from being poor. With education, they can help themselves, their families, their communities, their nations, and the planet.

However, millions of children around the world have limited access to education, because they live in remote places without funds for schools or easy access for families to get kids to school. Access to electricity might be limited, too.

Imagine that you live in a remote place without a school. Brainstorm ideas for creating one. Include solar or wind energy to provide electricity. Will your school include technology, such as computers? Also, think about how kids will get to the school.

GET CREATIVE. DRAW YOUR IDEAS HERE.

ACTIVISTS ARE BRAVE

What does it mean to be brave? It can mean doing something very dangerous like fighting a dragon. Usually, though, being brave means doing something much quieter and more personal than that. An act of bravery can mean being kind to someone in need. Even a smile for someone who is having a hard day can make a big difference. Saying "HELLO" to someone who is sitting alone at lunch or asking someone to play can be an act of bravery. So is standing up when someone is being picked on or speaking up when you see something wrong being done.

It is not easy to be brave, but it can make all the difference to someone else. Sofia had to be brave to help Abuelo. That was hard for her. She learned that being brave means doing the thing you must do, even if you're nervous and afraid.

Sofia also learned that being brave sets an example for other people to be brave, too.

Write about a time when you helped someone or did an act of kindness. A time when you were brave.

_____

_____

_____

_____

_____

_____

_____

_____

_____

_____

_____

_____

_____

_____

_____

WHERE DOES THE COMMUNITY'S MONEY COME FROM?

If you want to help your community, it's important to first understand how your community works. Communities are complicated. They involve lots of people working together.

The local government of a community works very hard to meet the needs of the people who live there. It is very important work. Thank a government worker when you meet them. They are working for you!

Even a space town in the distant future requires money to run. Like everyone, a town's employees need to support their families and buy groceries. School buildings, fire trucks, traffic lights, heat, air conditioning, parks, pothole patches, and flying trash trucks all require money.

But where does the money come from? The answer is taxes.

People can pay taxes from various sources: sales tax on items purchased, income tax on money earned, or property tax on the value of their homes. When you buy a candy bar, you pay a few cents extra in taxes. That money is how we pay for the things we value as a society. People and businesses pitch in together and use that money to take care of the community and one another.

Without taxes, we wouldn't have public schools or libraries, roads or bridges. We'd all have to buy our own fire trucks and flying trash trucks. It would be cool to have a flying trash truck, but it would also be too expensive for most people to afford. Pitching in together lets us pay for things that help us all.

Tax money helps pay your classroom teacher and fix the big pothole at the end of your street. It pays the people who will put out a fire or help you in an emergency.

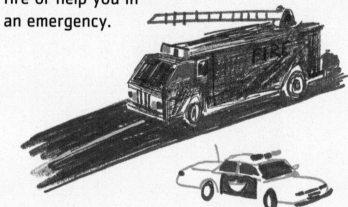

Look around your community. What things do you see that are paid for with tax money? Draw them here.

THE BUDGET ON GLORG

All the services, programs, buildings, equipment, and expenses in your community are paid for by taxes. Taxes are how citizens support the town and services they need and want.

THE SPENDING PLAN FOR A TOWN IS CALLED A BUDGET. TOWNS HAVE THREE KINDS OF BUDGET EXPENSES:

- **FIXED**—Expenses that are required for the health, safety, and education of the citizens and simply to run the town.

- **FLEXIBLE**—Expenses that are required at a basic level, but which can be increased to provide better services to the citizens.

- **OPTIONAL**—Expenses that are not required for basic citizen needs, but which add a lot to the town and make it a better place to live.

Running a town is very hard. As town leader, there is never enough money to do all the things you need and want to do. Sometimes, you have to make tough choices.

Imagine that you live in the distant future on the planet Glorg. Money on Glorg is called glorgins. Your town raised 150 glorgins through taxes. (It's a lot of space moolah!) As the town leader, you must figure out how to spend it.

Determine your budget using the chart on the next page. How much of each item does your town need? Do you have enough glorgins in your funds to cover all the items your town needs?

Get creative and think of new ways citizens can help the town without costing more glorgins. Brainstorm new, creative ways to raise more glorgins.

BRAINSTORM HERE:

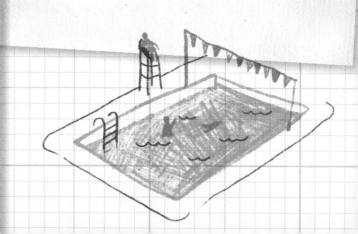

46

EXAMPLE:
Park Bench costs: 1 Glorgin x 3 Quantity = 3 Glorgins in Total Budget Item

	Budget Item	Cost (in Glorgins)	Quantity	Total for Budget Item
FIXED	City Hall maintenance	5	1	5
	City Employee salaries (at least 5 employees needed)	5		
	School buildings (at least 2 needed)	5		
	Teacher salary (at least 4 teachers needed per school)	5		
	Library	10	1	10
	Public safety services and staff	25	1	25
	Sewer maintenance	5	1	5
FLEXIBLE	Streetlight (1 per road is best. There are 10 roads.)	5		
	City parks and maintenance (at most 5 parks possible)	5		
	Road maintenance (There are 10 roads. Maintenance is important, but not mandatory.)	2		
OPTIONAL	City swimming pool	10		
	Lifeguard salary (at least 2 guards required per pool)	2		
	Zoo	10		
	Monkey, Llama, and Zebra food	3		
	Hippo food (They are hungry, hungry hippos.)	3		
	Summer concerts (Citizens love these! 5 per summer is desired by citizens. Concerts require at least one park.)	2		
	Fireworks (require at least one park)	5		
	Parade (requires at least 2 maintained roads)	1		
	Park Bench (3 required per open park)	1		
	Water park	10		
	Sports fields for baseball, soccer, tennis	5		
	Other:			
TOTAL BUDGET				

ACTIVISTS ARE GOOD LISTENERS

Activists try to help others. But first, they must understand what other people care about and the problems they face. To do that, activists must be good listeners.

Listening to others is one of the most important things you can do in life. Unfortunately, many people are very bad at it! The first lesson in being a good listener is to remember that you can't listen and talk at the same time!

As you have conversations about topics you care about, listen to others. Make a list here of concerns you hear from others over one week.

SUNDAY
_____

MONDAY
_____

TUESDAY
_____

WEDNESDAY
_____

THURSDAY
_____

FRIDAY
_____

SATURDAY

ACTIVISTS ARE GOOD COMMUNICATORS

Real change begins when people come together one-to-one and understand each other through conversation. Having meaningful conversations is more than just talking. You need to ask questions, listen to the answers, and think of more questions and observations. When both people in a conversation do these things, each person learns about the other person and shares something about themselves and what is important to them.

BEING GOOD AT CONVERSATIONS TAKES PRACTICE AND EFFORT. HERE ARE SOME RULES AND IDEAS TO HELP YOU:

1. Pay attention. Look at the person who is talking with you. It shows respect and helps you understand what they are saying better.

2. Listen. Really and truly listen to the other person. Listening is not just hearing. It means thinking about what the other person says.

3. Ask questions. "What?" "Why?" "How?"

4. Listen to the answers. Take an interest in them.

5. In your own words, try to sum up what the other person said. This shows that you understood what they said. If you don't completely understand, this is a great time to ask them to explain what they mean. The best communicators say when they don't understand something. (It's how they learn!) Once you under-stand, continue to the next step.

6. Ask a question about something you learned in the answer.

7. Repeat that process of asking questions and listening to the answers.

8. From time to time, connect their answers with things you know. Share your connections.

9. Ask more questions! Always be willing to say "I don't know" or "Could you explain that?"

The focus of every conversation should be understanding the other person!

The best conversations happen when both parties ask questions, listen to the answers, and add connections.

Each person focuses on the other person. As the conversation grows, common interests and ideas become clear.

It sounds easy, but it takes practice!

Find a friend to practice your conversation skills with.

MAKE NOTES ABOUT THINGS YOU LEARNED

EVERYONE CAN DO SOMETHING

Activism is not somebody else's job.
Remember: Nobody can do everything. But everyone can do something.

Think about something you can do today to make the world a better place.
It can be a small thing or a big thing.

WRITE ABOUT IT HERE OR DRAW A PICTURE

CONTACT YOUR OFFICIALS

It is important for elected officials to hear from the people they represent.
It helps them know when they are helping their communities and when they can do better.
It can also bring issues to their attention.

WHEN YOU WRITE TO YOUR ELECTED OFFICIAL, ALWAYS:

1. Be respectful.

2. Be clear and to the point. They are busy people!

3. Spell their names correctly.

4. Thank them for their time and consideration.

Here is a sample letter you can use to help you craft a letter to your elected official.

Date [Month Day, Year]

Address [Mayor/Representative/Senator/Governor/President Name]

Dear [Mayor/Representative/Senator/Governor/President],

My name is [NAME], and I am writing to you from [TOWN] to share my concern about [ISSUE]. [ISSUE] is important to me because [HOW IT AFFECTS YOU*]. This is very important because it [WHY IT MATTERS*].

I hope that you can help find a solution to [ISSUE*]. I believe it will improve our [TOWN, STATE, COUNTRY].

Thank you for your attention and time.

Sincerely,

[Signature]

*You can expand on these sections to explain the problem and possible solutions.

PRACTICE WRITING TO YOUR OFFICIAL HERE:

Dear _____,

_____

_____

_____

_____

_____

Thank you for your attention and time.

Sincerely,

_____

Dear Mr. Mayor,

My name is Sofia Valdez. I am a second grader at Blue River Creek Elementary School. I am very concerned about the large trash heap in town. Abuelo was hurt yesterday at Mount Trashmore. I am worried that other people might get hurt, too. I believe that we could improve Blue River Creek by turning this dangerous mess into a park where everyone could gather and play. I have many ideas about the park and hope to share them with you. Thank you for all you do to help our community.

Sincerely,

Sofia Valdez

REAL-WORLD PROBLEMS

The cost of houses or apartments in many cities in the world is very high. This means that many people cannot afford to live in the city centers where they work. Instead, they drive, which adds to traffic, road construction, and the burning of fossil fuel, which adds to the climate crisis.*

The problem is complex. Brainstorm ideas for affordable housing and transportation in a big city. How could we make housing and transportation more accessible to more people? Could bike lanes help people get around? What about subways or elevated trains? Could the city offer affordable apartments for people with low income?

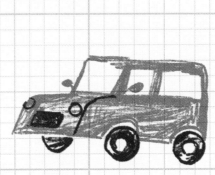

* Learn about fossil fuels and climate change in
Ada Twist's Big Project Book for Stellar Scientists.

THINK ABOUT ENERGY SOURCES AND MATERIALS FOR HOUSING AND TRANSPORTATION. GET CREATIVE. DRAW YOUR IDEAS HERE.

ACTIVISTS
ARE CREATIVE

The Government of Blue River Creek loved Sofia's idea to combine the library and the zoo. The new branch of the library at the zoo has been a big hit with the citizens of Blue River Creek AND the animals. However, there are also some problems to work out. The biggest problem is the giraffes. They love to eat the green books, which remind them of leaves. No matter how high up or low down the librarian puts the green books, the giraffes find a way to get them.

+

There are many ways to solve a problem. Often, just thinking about the problem in a new way can help you find a solution.

Can you create two solutions to the problem? Make the solutions as different from each other as possible. (Feel free to think of the people and the zoo animals as part of your solutions.)

SOLUTION ONE

SOLUTION TWO

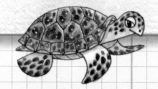

ACTIVISTS ARE PATIENT

Progress rarely comes in one big step. More often, it is made through small steps, constant work, and struggle over years, decades, and even centuries. It is easy to feel frustrated, but change happens when people keep working hard for a cause in which they believe.

For example, when the United States Constitution was adopted in 1789, only white, property-owning men could vote. It was not until 1965 that voting rights were protected for all U.S. citizens no matter their race, gender, or religion. For more than 176 years, people struggled, suffered, and even died for the right to vote. Never forget that!

TIMELINE OF VOTING RIGHTS EXPANSION IN THE UNITED STATES

1789   The U.S. Constitution is adopted. Voting is limited to white, male landowners.

1856   Property ownership requirement ends. All white men are allowed to vote.

1868   The Fourteenth Amendment grants Black men U.S. citizenship but not the right to vote.

1870   The Fifteenth Amendment makes it so that federal and state governments cannot deny citizens the right to vote based on race, color, or on previously being a slave. Black men have the right to vote, but some states and local governments use voting taxes, literacy tests, and other rules to keep them from voting.

1920   The Nineteenth Amendment gives women the right to vote. This rule mostly applies to white women. Many Black women are prevented from voting by voting taxes, literacy tests, and other rules. Not all Native American and Asian women have citizenship.

1924   Indian Citizenship Act. Native Americans have full citizenship, but some states prevent them from voting through taxes, literacy tests, and other discriminatory rules.

1952   The McCarran-Walter Act grants all people of Asian ancestry the right to become citizens and vote.

1961   The Twenty-third Amendment grants Washington, D.C., residents the right to vote for the president, but they have no congressional representation.

1965   Voting Rights Act forbids states from making restrictions that discriminate against voters. All minorities who have been kept from voting by such laws are given voting protection by the federal government.

Make a list of big changes you would like to see in the world during your lifetime. Add to the list when you think of something new. Note smaller changes you see happening or read about in the news.

ACTIVISTS ARE VIGILANT

That means they keep careful watch. Sometimes, progress that has been made to help people can be reversed. When this happens, activists and others need to pay attention and keep working to make more progress.

For example, in the United States, progress made in voting rights has been reversed in some places, making it harder or impossible for people to vote. This is called voter suppression. It can be done in lots of ways. Sometimes, people's names are taken off voter rolls for reasons that don't make sense. Or places where people are supposed to vote are closed down or moved to make it harder for people to get there. The hours available for voting may be limited.

Contact the local government department in charge of voting in your community and learn what you can about voting registration and rules. What is the process for being able to vote? Are there restrictions on who can vote? How can you learn who is running in an election? Where and when does voting take place?

Share what you learn with people you know who are eligible to vote. Encourage them to get registered and vote.

MAKE NOTES HERE ABOUT WHAT YOU LEARN:

I VOTED

ACTIVISTS ARE HUMBLE*

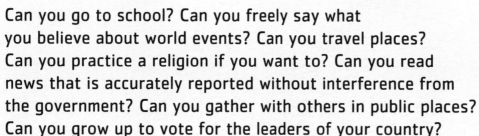

Think about the things that you have the freedom to do.

Can you go to school? Can you freely say what you believe about world events? Can you travel places? Can you practice a religion if you want to? Can you read news that is accurately reported without interference from the government? Can you gather with others in public places? Can you grow up to vote for the leaders of your country?

Many people around the planet do not have all of these rights. If you can do any of these things, it is because people who came before you struggled, fought, and sometimes even died for these rights. Their sacrifices and hard work make all of our lives better.

Never, ever forget what others have done to make your life and the world better.

Ask your librarian for books about people who have worked to make the world a better place. Learn about activists from as many places around the world as you can.

DRAW A PICTURE OF OR WRITE ABOUT SOMEONE WHO HAS CHANGED THE WORLD HERE.

*Being humble means not having an excess of pride in yourself. Even though having pride in yourself is very important, having too much can keep you from recognizing the value of other people's contributions.

REAL-WORLD PROBLEMS

Look around you right now. Do you see anything made of plastic?

Chances are, there is plastic all around you. Some items made of plastic are used for a long time. But others are used only one time before ending up in the trash. Plastic straws, cups, and grocery bags are examples of single-use plastics.

In many ways, plastic makes life easier for people. However, an enormous amount of plastic finds its way to the ocean, where it breaks down into tiny bits. These microplastics are ingested by sea life. Microplastics can be toxic to animals and fish and to the other animals and fish who eat them. That includes people!

1. Look around you. Count the items near you that include single-use plastic. Write down the number you see.

2. Observe your family's habits for a week. Can you cut down on the single-use plastics in your life? Think about replacing, reusing, recycling, and avoiding single-use plastics. Make a list of ways you can reduce your use.

Eight **MILLION** tons of plastic waste are swept from land into the sea every year. (That does not include the amount that is dumped directly from ships or during natural disasters like hurricanes or tsunamis!)

Even plastic far from the ocean can end up in the ocean. Litter and trash that is not properly handled blows across the land and is swept by rain into small creeks or streams. Creeks and streams lead to rivers, and ultimately, out to the ocean.

WHAT CAN YOU DO TO STOP PLASTIC FROM GETTING INTO THE OCEAN?

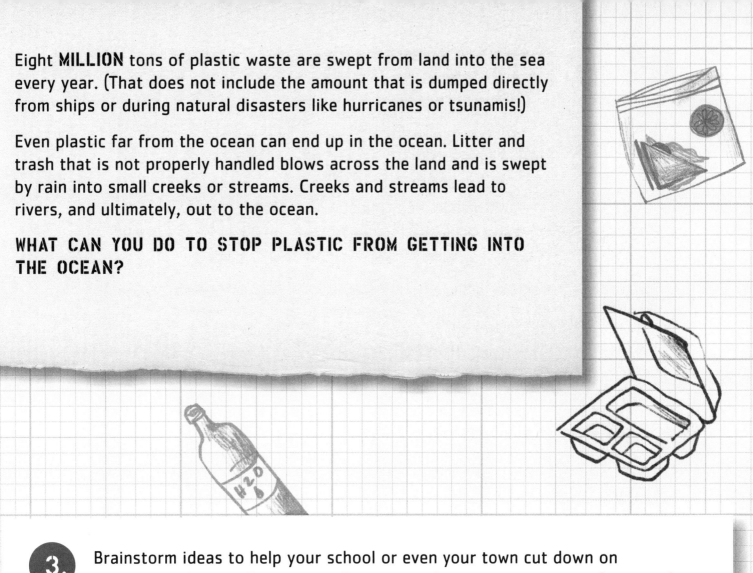

3. Brainstorm ideas to help your school or even your town cut down on single-use plastics. Be creative. Draw your ideas or write a story if you prefer.

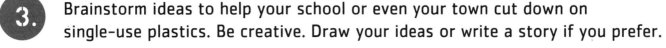

ACTIVISTS ARE KIND

Activism begins with kindness.

It begins when someone sees another person who needs assistance and says,
"HOW CAN I HELP?"

An act of kindness can be as simple as a smile or a kind word.
Sitting at recess with someone who is lonely, or simply listening to someone
who is worried or upset.

Each act of kindness is like the tiny splash of a pebble thrown into a pond.
It sends waves in wider and wider and wider circles.

Each act of kindness can inspire others to also be kind and to work together
to change things that need changing. Those people inspire even more people.
If they all work together, big changes can happen!

SOMETHING KIND

You can help to change the world

with your deeds. Your heart. Your mind.

Just remember, when you act,

to start with something kind.

Draw a picture or write about a time when you did something kind.

ACTIVISTS HARNESS THEIR EMOTIONS TO HELP OTHERS

For instance, anger is a natural emotion. Everybody experiences it. Anger can be very powerful, but it can also be harmful.

When Abuelo fell at Mount Trashmore and hurt his ankle, Sofia was scared and sad. The next day, as she walked home, Sofia got very angry.

When Sofia got angry about the trash heap, she also had a choice to make. She could choose to stay angry. Or, she could choose to use that energy to make a difference and do something positive. Sofia chose to make a difference. She got busy and turned that negative energy into positive action to help Abuelo and all the people in Blue River Creek who needed a place to gather.

Think of a time when you were very angry. Find a way to make something positive using the energy from your anger. Create a dance! Make a sculpture from clay or dough! Make music! Make art! Plant a flower! Brainstorm ideas of how you can fix the problem that made you angry!

WRITE ABOUT IT HERE:

_____

_____

_____

_____

_____

_____

_____

_____

_____

ACTIVISTS GET INFORMED

There is always help at the library. Libraries have thousands and thousands
of books to read, but they also have lots of other resources. Libraries have computers,
magazines, video libraries, and services to help people find a job. Some even have
social workers to help people. Call your library and ask to meet with a librarian who
can show you some of the amazing resources at the library!

LIST THEM HERE:

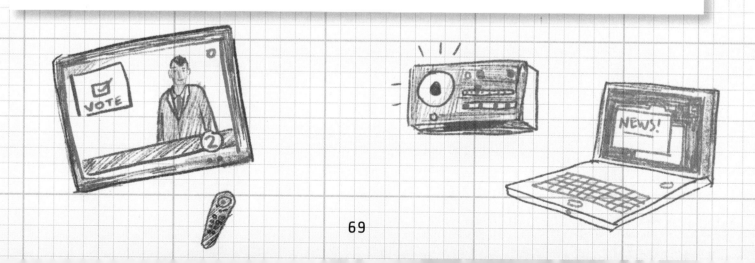

KNOW YOUR COMMUNITY

When you turn on the faucet, water comes out. Where does it come from? Who makes sure it is available? Who makes sure it is clean?

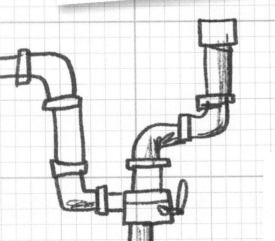

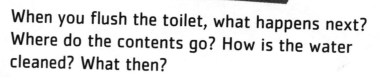

When you flush the toilet, what happens next? Where do the contents go? How is the water cleaned? What then?

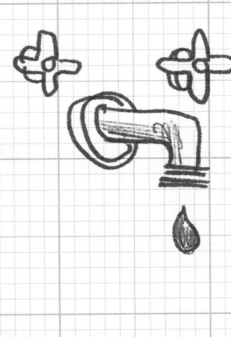

Learn what you can about these questions!
Write or draw about it here.

MARCHING WITH SIGNS

The students in Miss Lila Greer's class showed their support for Sofia's cause by marching with signs. The signs had catchy slogans to attract people's attention and spread awareness about the new park.

Think about a problem you want to help people understand. Create some signs for a rally here.

ACTIVISTS READ, QUESTION, AND THINK!

Every person needs to understand what is going on in their community, town, region, nation, and planet! It's not somebody else's job!

We rely on journalists to tell us the
"WHO, WHAT, WHEN, WHERE, WHY, AND HOW"
of events. Journalists share their findings in print, online, on television, on the radio, and in other formats. A librarian can help you find reliable news sources that report honestly.

A journalist's job is to report the truth. That means accurately reporting facts. They must make sure the facts can be proven. Journalists also give facts a context so people can understand them. Journalists' loyalty is to the readers, not to the people who pay their salaries, or who print their work, or who have political or other kinds of power.

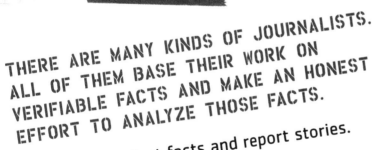

THERE ARE MANY KINDS OF JOURNALISTS. ALL OF THEM BASE THEIR WORK ON VERIFIABLE FACTS AND MAKE AN HONEST EFFORT TO ANALYZE THOSE FACTS.

- Reporters collect facts and report stories.

- Columnists write articles with their point of view on a topic.

- Editorial cartoonists use art and often humor to express an opinion on a news event.

- Editorial writers express the views of the publication on a topic.

BLUE RIVER CREEK DAILY NEWS

– Since 1879 –

TODAY IN POLITICS

SOFIA VALDEZ, FUTURE PRESIDENT!

_____ _____

_____ _____

_____ _____

_____ _____

_____ _____

_____ _____

2. **BE A COLUMNIST.** Newspapers and other news sources often have opinion writers who think about a news event and share what they think about the events. They aim to use facts and reason to develop a thoughtful opinion. Try writing an opinion piece about Sofia Valdez. (Some sample opinion topics: Sofia and Abuelo are trespassers at the landfill. The Clerk is great at her job because she listened to Sofia and got others to listen, too. Sofia is a bad dog owner for giving Pup cookies and letting him chase squirrels. The mayor is anti-kid.)

BLUE RIVER CREEK DAILY NEWS

YOUR HEADLINE HERE

YOUR AD HERE

3. MAKE AN ADVERTISEMENT.
Newspapers include advertisements for products and services companies offer. Create an advertisement for one of the stores you might find in Blue River Creek.

4. BE AN ARTIST.
Editorial cartoons can be very simple, but powerful. Create an editorial cartoon about something that happened in the story.

BLUE RIVER CREEK DAILY NEWS
Page 3

YOUR EDITORIAL CARTOONS HERE

AN IMPORTANT NOTE ABOUT THE FREE PRESS!

A free press means that the government cannot control what is reported. A free press acts like a watchdog and helps citizens know when their officials are doing their jobs well and when they are not. It can even reveal abuses of power and illegal actions.

News sources that uphold the principles of good journalism help citizens understand what is happening. However, not all news sources do this. Some distort the truth or spread false information. They can do this by reporting incorrect information or by leaving out important information.

Being a journalist is hard work. It can also be dangerous work. In many countries, a journalist who disagrees with the government or who reports on the government's bad actions can be attacked, thrown in prison, or worse. Freedom of the press is a right that can be lost if it is not protected.

Beware of anyone who ever calls the free press an "enemy of the people." These words have been used by tyrants and bad leaders for centuries. They are powerful and dangerous words meant to make people stop trusting facts. Once the people stop believing facts, they are easy to fool. People who are easily fooled are easily taken advantage of by bad leaders. That is when democracy fails. That is when fear and violence govern instead of laws. Always be suspicious of a leader who says this!

A NOTE ABOUT THE VOTE!

The most important things an activist can do are to understand how the government works by always being informed, and to participate in whatever way they can to make the government run better.

This means voting if you can! You might be too young to vote in an election now, but very soon, you will be old enough.

HERE ARE SOME IMPORTANT THINGS TO REMEMBER AND TO SHARE WITH PEOPLE YOU KNOW WHO VOTE:

- **Voting has consequences.** Voting gives you a say in what happens in your community, city, state, and country. Elections can even affect the planet! You must be informed and vote wisely.

- **Not voting also has consequences.** If you don't vote, you give up your power to make change. AND you give your power to the people who *do* vote. Can you be sure they want the same things you want or need?

- **Voting honors those who fought for your right to vote.** History is filled with people who struggled, sacrificed, and even died for the right to vote. Respect that.

- **Even if an election doesn't affect you very much, the outcome could be very important to others in your community.** Get informed and think about how your vote could help children, the homeless, or other groups who might not have a voice. Your vote can make a difference in their lives. Use your power to help them.

- **Prepare to vote now by learning all you can about your community, city, state, country, and planet.** Make a habit of being informed. Seek out reliable news sources every day. Read. Question. Think. That's your job.

CAMPAIGN SIGNS

Imagine you are running for office. For a campaign, it is helpful to have a slogan:
a short, catchy phrase people will remember that describes an important idea.
For instance: "**ONWARD TOGETHER**"; "**NOT ME, US**"; "**DREAM BIG, FIGHT HARD.**"

What would your campaign slogan be? Create a sign here asking people to vote for you.

ACTIVISTS ARE GENEROUS

Activists care about other people and are generous with their time, energy, talents, and other resources. Keep a set of lists here of your talents, interests, and opportunities. The lists will grow over time!

THINGS YOU ARE GOOD AT

(examples: talking to people, listening to others, dancing, taking care of animals, sewing, running, bicycling, crochet or knitting, drawing, working hard, reading books, handwriting . . .)

TOPICS THAT INTEREST YOU
(animals, helping kids, the environment, homelessness . . .)

SPECIFIC NEEDS IN YOUR COMMUNITY
(kitty litter at an animal shelter, gardening help at a senior center, greeting cards welcoming new students to school, food donations to a local food pantry . . .)

VOLUNTEER OPPORTUNITIES IN YOUR COMMUNITY

Ask your librarian, teacher, parent, or other adult you respect to help you find suitable groups in your community.

IDEAS OF NEW WAYS YOU MIGHT BE ABLE TO HELP!

Think how you can use your talents to help. Be creative!

Get your friends involved. It's more fun together!

ACTIVISTS ARE LEADERS!

Write each characteristic in the diagram below:

INSPIRING, BRAVE, GOOD LISTENERS, EMPATHETIC, GOOD COMMUNICATORS, WORK WELL WITH OTHERS, CREATIVE, PATIENT, HUMBLE, VIGILANT, GENEROUS.

Which characteristics describe an activist? Which describe a leader? Which describe both?

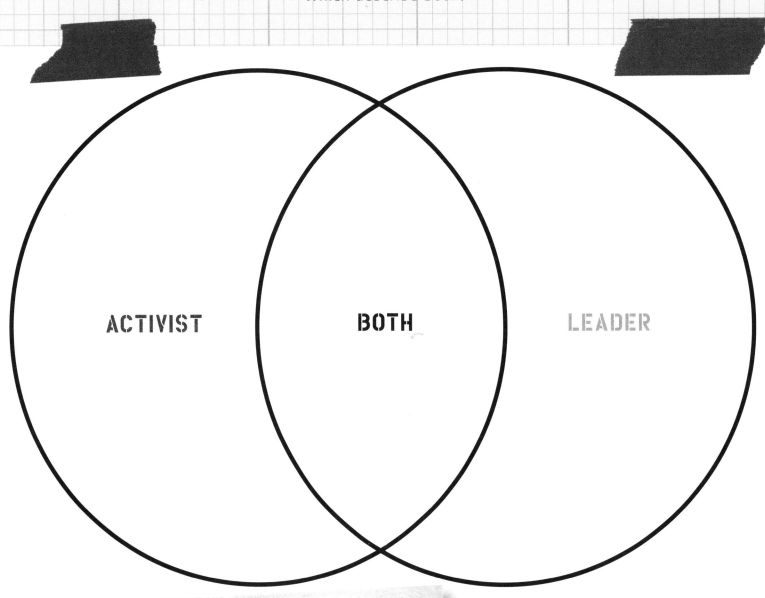

ACTIVIST

BOTH

LEADER

Making the world a better place is not somebody else's job. Nobody can do everything to fix the problems of the world, but everyone can do something. What can you do?

HOW TO MAKE YOUR OWN POSTER FOR MARCHES

1. Cut out this page and page 92.

2. Glue the pages to either side of a piece of cardboard. If desired, attach a paint stirrer or stick to use as a handle.

BE AN ACTIVIST.
READ.
QUESTION.
THINK.

THE QUESTIONEERS

QUESTIONEERS.COM

ABRAMS

SEA UNA ACTIVISTA.
LEA.
PREGUNTE.
PIENSE.

THE QUESTIONEERS

By Andrea Beaty, Illustrations © David Roberts

QUESTIONEERS.COM

ABRAMS

CUT OUT THIS PAGE

When you are tired or frightened or weary or scared, remember this:

YOU ARE BRAVER THAN YOU KNOW AND MIGHTIER THAN YOU CAN EVER IMAGINE. BE BOLD.

Draw your wonderful, beautiful, astonishing, fabulous, amazing face here.

SOLUTION TO ACTIVIST'S WORD SEARCH

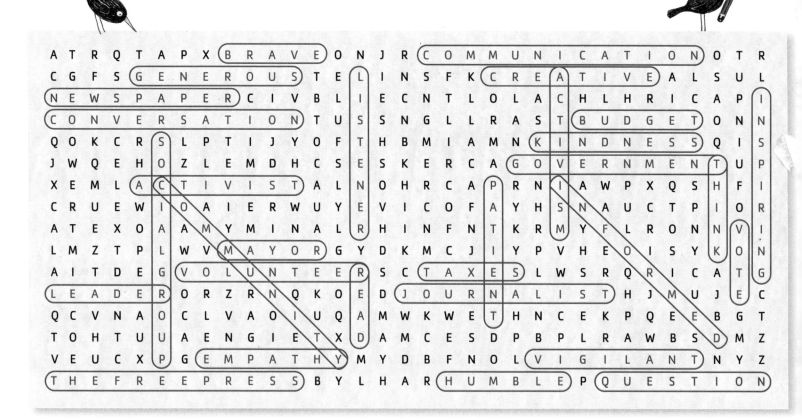

Activist	Inspiring	Read	Brave
Activism	Budget	Question	Patient
Community	Taxes	Think	Creative
Government	Listener	Informed	Vigilant
Vote	Conversation	Newspaper	Humble
Leader	Communication	Journalist	Empathy
Generous	Kindness	The Free Press	
Mayor	Volunteer	Social Group	